THE HUNTING ROOKIE

***

How a Mentor and a Thirst for Adventure

Bred a Late Start Hunter

***

Bert J. Rico

Published by D&L Books LLC

ISBN: 978-1-7349419-0-6 (paperback)
ISBN: 978-1-7349419-1-3 (ebook)

First Edition

"To truly leave a legacy and forever leave a mark on this world, you should do three things. You should plant a tree, have kids, and write a book."

- Martha Inez "Iya" Alvarez

Special thank you firstly to my wife, for being the best partner I could have ever dreamt of and for putting up with my terrible habit of buying camping and hunting gear.

Also thank you to my mom for being my number 1 supporter and really encouraging me to write this book despite her not being a fan of hunting herself.

Finally thank you to Uncle Manny. If it weren't for you, I would have never truly discovered my passion for the outdoors, wildlife, and conservation. Thank you for taking me on my first outdoors adventure and always willing to be a part of my future ones.

To The Reader

Thank you so much for purchasing and reading this book. It has been a lifelong goal to write one and if you enjoyed reading it as much as I enjoyed writing it, it would be a great help if you added a review on Amazon and/or Goodreads. For more content and information on this or upcoming books, be sure to follow me on Instagram @theHuntingRookie.

Contents

Preface

I have learned that everyone loves a good story, and hunting stories are the oldest kind. For as long as we have been telling them or folk tales, myths, and fables, there have been stories about hunters in one form or another. The best ones usually are told around a campfire. The best kind of hunting story, I would argue, is a bad one. Now I don't mean a poorly told story. No, what I mean is a story of a hunt gone wrong, or one with insurmountable challenges.

Preface

There is more joy and laughter, for both the narrator and the audience, in the telling of the giant buck that outsmarted the hunter and got away, than there is in the trophy buck that was harvested on the first day of the hunter's first hunt of the season. I would venture to say that the suckiest experience at the time really turns into the better story later. The badge of honor you feel in coming out of the other side of that hard fought, emotional roller coaster encounter, is always bigger and brighter than a lucky one.

The best overall experience for a hunter is when they are going through their worst hunt. For us south-eastern hunters, it's the abnormally hot and humid November, with the largest birth rate of mosquitos in a generation swarming even the red glow of our head lamps. It's the one with no visible sign of your quarry anywhere, but despite that, you stick it out anyway. You tough the discomfort and misery. You persist and persevere, and you are rewarded with a successful hunt on your last day.

That feeling. Oh, that feeling right there, is a feeling that is so incredibly hard to describe in words and that few can ever really understand.

The flood of emotions that wash over you in an instant has a different effect on everyone. Some shake violently, some can't seem to catch their breath, some just sit motionless and speechless, some yip and yell in a burst of energy that can't be contained, and some a combination of those.

The most common question I get asked by non-hunters, is why I hunt. It's always asked in varied intonations and with varying agendas. Some are genuinely curious, and perhaps have fantasized about hunting one day themselves. Others are aimed with pointed accuracy and have the weight of a thousand elephants in the room. I do my best to answer both as honestly and unabashedly as possible. However, it remains a tough one to answer. It seems strange how something I feel so passionately about could be so difficult to answer. I can spout the benefits of conservation, which I absolutely believe in. I do feel that our North American model of conservation is the best in the world, but that is a justification and not a reason. I can say that the animals live a better life in the wild before they are hunted than they ever would in a ranch or farm. Again, another justification. I can even say it is the most natural, organic, and pure way to feed my family, but that feels more like a rationalization. I think why we hunt as a community is difficult to define because it is so heavily based on emotion and that emotion is so different from one hunter to the next.

Similarly, our ethics are so varied as a community for the same reason. To make things even more complicated and as straightforward as a bowl of spaghetti, I have found that a hunter's reason for hunting, as well as their ethics may change over time. As one grows and experiences more, it is common for perspectives and opinions to change. Because of this, I can't speak for the entire community, but only for myself and only for myself at the time of writing this book.

I hunt because it makes me feel connected to something, something I think we lost as a society and as a culture. It's not this innate blood thirst I am trying to quench, nothing even remotely in that realm. It's a connection to the natural order of things. It's a connection I feel with varied degrees of intensity, and that I feel whether I am successful or not. When reading this explanation as words on a paper, I realize it is difficult to comprehend. There are those reading though, who most likely are hunters, and can fully understand the emotion that washes over you. The emotion that ebbs and flows in ups and downs throughout your hunt. It's not about pulling the trigger. It's not about the taking of a life. It's not even about the meat harvested. It's about all of it. All of it, and this invisible connection to the animal you are hunting, the land you are hunting, and the history and tradition of hunting. It's

Preface

a connection you can't explain but can only experience.

Chapter 1: Eager Rookie

I had spent all day looking at my watch. My leg shaking up and down in rapid succession at my eagerness for the clock to hit 5PM. To pass the time, I had watched every possible video I could find on how to field dress an animal, how to butcher an animal, and recipes to make for wild boar. I know, I know, don't count your chickens before they hatch and all that, but I couldn't help myself. At 5PM I was on my way to my first ever hunting trip and I couldn't wait. Needless to say, it was not a very productive day for me at work.

Chapter 1: Eager Rookie

I have always dreamt what it would be like to go hunting. I have read books about the adventures of men like Theodore Roosevelt and Lewis and Clark and often fantasized about being on an expedition with them. Even as a child in grade school, I read books like *The Adventures of Huckleberry Finn,* and *The Indian in the Cupboard,* and always found myself especially drawn in when the authors described things like the use of snares, or building shelters from materials found in the woods. There was always this glamour I saw in anything the broached the subject of living off the land and being close to nature.

As far as outdoors experiences before hunting I had, of course, gone fishing off the coast of Miami, FL with my dad quite a few times. Few native Miamians haven't. Heck, I even had a fishing trip to Bimini in the Bahamas under my belt. There just something about hunting though that brought back all those childhood daydreams of being a pioneer and living off the land. I also have a passion for cooking for my family. One of the biggest rewards of those childhood fishing trips, besides being on the water, was the meal that came after and was shared with the entire family. Of course, those meals were filled with often exaggerated accounts of the experience, the fight of the fish, the number of fish caught, and the size of the biggest catch of the day.

I had created in my mind, a picture of what it would be like to go hunting and prepare a family meal where the main portion of the dish was harvested by me and was prepared, truly, from start to finish. While fishing is almost a religion in Miami. You could toss a penny in the air and would have a real good chance of it hitting a fisherman on the way down, but finding a hunter was much more challenging and was another matter entirely. I never really had anyone to go with. Much less someone show me the ropes. My family wasn't very outdoorsy at all and my dad absolutely preferred to

Chapter 1: Eager Rookie

be on the water than spend any time out in the woods or swamp.

It wasn't until I got married and had my son that I met Uncle Manny. He is my brother in law's, girlfriend's father. I know a freakin' mouthful. He has become one of my closest friends and my son has known him his whole life and affectionately calls him Uncle Manny. The name stuck and now that's all he is known by throughout our family.

Uncle Manny is older than me by 20 or so years. He is about 5' 10" and while he is now heavy set, his broad shoulders and barrel chest are testament to his previous fitness and musculature in his Army days. He has thick black hair and a thick goatee that are both sprinkled with flecks of silver here and there. At first sight you can get a sense of his no-nonsense personality, and only those lucky enough to be in his inner circle get to know that contagious sense of humor, and his sarcasm which is second to none. Most people are intimidated by him when meeting him for the first time, but for some strange reason, kids are a different story. They flock to him and seem to immediately be comfortable with him. He has the attention of my son whenever we go over.

Uncle Manny has been an avid big game hunter throughout his life. When I discovered this, I would ask him question after question on his experiences. One of the stories that stuck in my head the most was a bear hunt he did in Canada with an outfitter. They had to ride horses into their hunting area and packed the meat out on horseback as well. He recounted that hunt with not only the details of the hunt itself, but the experience of sleeping in a log cabin that had none of today's modern-day comforts like electricity, insulation, or running water. He told me about the homemade food that was cooked up on a primitive wood burning stove that had been like nothing he had tasted before. As he continued to describe what it had been like, all I could think of was how amazing it must have been,

Chapter 1: Eager Rookie

and how much I wanted an experience like that. Where I had a candle light's worth of curiosity for hunting, Uncle Manny came by and doused that small flame with gasoline. The burning desire to hunt just continued to grow.

Not long after, I started to research first hunts, requirements for hunting, and basically consumed as much information as I could. I was still apprehensive as to whether I would like wild game or not, or if I would really enjoy the experience or if I had just built up this hype in my mind so much that it would turn out to be nowhere near as exciting as I imagined.

In my research, I discovered that in Florida, no hunting license is required when hunting on private land for wild boar. I figured I can find an outfitter that would allow me to hunt on private property and see if I really do like it before committing 100% to gear and a hunting license. Hours of google searches over several days later and I found one that looked promising. I copied down the link and messaged it to Uncle Manny. I figured if he was interested in going with me, I would figure out logistics on the trip later.

That same evening, I got his reply. Not only was he in, but he had a good friend that lived minutes away in Fort McCoy, FL and we could stay with him. He would even be interested in tagging along. I couldn't believe it. He called his friend Leon and he didn't hesitate either. Everything was quickly arranged and in less than 2 months' time, I would be on my first ever hunting trip.

Chapter 2: An Intro to a New Hunter

The day was finally here. I was working from home that day and had my bag packed and ready to go by the door. Uncle Manny told me that he would be at my house at 5:00PM sharp and we would hit the road right away, no lollygagging. If you knew Uncle Manny, you would know he wasn't kidding. He may be retired from the Army, but there is nothing retired about his military discipline. He would leave me behind in a heartbeat if I wasn't ready.

All day I could do nothing but think about this hunt. Re-watching field dressing videos I had seen at least 10 times already. I handled whatever questions came my way on my work messaging app and tried to complete a task or two before I had to leave but my brain just wasn't in it. 4:58 PM and Uncle Manny was knocking at my door. As soon as I opened it, he looked at me with a crooked smile and asked me,

"You all set?"

"Just about, let me shutdown my PC and put an out of office reply on my email." I replied.

He reached down to where my bag was lying next to the door and said, "You got two minutes."

He then turned and walked toward his truck and tossed the bag in the back seat. I wrapped up my last email and by 5:01PM we were on the road. It

Chapter 2: An Intro to a New Hunter

was a 5-hour trip with only one stop in the middle for gas and dinner. We ended up getting there a little after 10:30PM.

Fort McCoy is a very small community in North Central, FL. There are very few streetlights and literally none when you turn off the main road to go down the street that Uncle Manny's friend Leon lived. I had never experienced a small town before. I had travelled of course, but always to big cities like New York and Boston. Right when we made this last turn Uncle Manny wanted to show me what "far" really meant in a town like this compared to what we were used to. He stopped his truck, looked over at me and said

"This is Leon's street and he is just up this road. Look at the time."

It was a little before 10PM. It took us almost 40 minutes of driving in the pitch black to get there. This may not sound like a big deal, but 40 minutes was my commute from home to work on the whole opposite side of the city back in Miami, assuming there was no traffic of course. This would be the commute for Leon just to get to the main road to then drive at least another 20 minutes just to get to a grocery store. An Hour drive just for groceries. There was no pizza delivery out here, and you had better make sure you didn't forget anything on your grocery list.

We finally made it to the front gate of Leon's property. We opened the gate and pulled in. directly in front of us was the main house, but he had a studio apartment built on the second floor of his Barn. We got there late and didn't want to wake them. Leon had also left us the key to the barn and the studio upstairs anyway. We off-loaded just our clothes and rifles and went upstairs. The studio had been prepared for us with fresh linens on the two queen sized beds on either side of the room. The furniture was this heavy solid wood that really made you feel like you were in a log cabin in the middle of

Chapter 2: An Intro to a New Hunter

the woods somewhere. The air conditioner was on full blast, so the room felt crisp and cool as soon as you walked in and blew a woody, almost nutty smell that was incredibly pleasant. Down a narrow hallway there was a full kitchen and bathroom complete with running water and a stand-up shower. It was one heck of a mancave to say the least. We were tired from the drive and decided to go right to sleep and try to be as well rested as we could for the next day.

***

We woke up the next morning at around 7AM. Out of respect for how nice Leon and his wife had left the studio for us we made our beds and swept up some of the dirt we had trekked in the night before. Even though we were up early, our outfitter was close-by and we had signed up for a half-day hunt in the afternoon through sundown. We had quite some time before we had to get going. We went downstairs to the main floor of the barn and walked over to the main house. Before we got to the door, Leon's wife Vicki, greeted and welcomed us in. She greeted Uncle Manny with a big hug that had the weight of the far too much time that had passed since their last meeting. She then greeted me with the same exact warmth, as if we had known each other for years even though we were only just officially meeting then.

Their home and property were beautiful. Coming in so late, we couldn't appreciate it the night before. In the darkness we could only just make out the shapes of the houses and barn on the property, but now we were able to take it all in. The house sits in the middle of the plot which was a little over 3 acres It bumps right up to the shores of Lake Ocklawaha which was visible from most of the property, but the best view was from the back patio.

The patio was probably my favorite feature. It was screened in, because well in Florida, it may sometimes feel like the mosquitos are equipped

Chapter 2: An Intro to a New Hunter

with swords. It ran the length of the back of the house with incredible views of the manicured lawn as it sloped down to the lake shore. The patio was furnished with rocking chairs and at the left most end, an outdoor dining area. From there, you could also see Leon's dock which housed a pontoon and an air boat which he used to fish the bass and panfish in the lake.

***

Fun fact about Lake Ocklawaha, it was originally the Ocklawaha river but in the early 1900s the Army corps of engineers was tasked with building a waterway that went from the Atlantic coast to the Gulf of Mexico. In 1961 they completed the Rodman Dam in service of this endeavor. However, due to legal trouble, President Richard Nixon abandoned the project and it has been left undone ever since. There have been some movements to remove the Rodman Dam to return the area back to its original riverbed, but none have gained any serious steam. If you ever get an opportunity to check out the lake, it is worth it. It's filled with gorgeous views, all sorts of wildlife, of course a healthy fish population, and is one of the most peaceful places I have ever experienced.

***

Across from where the lake meets their property is the road frontage, which is always quiet, and then there is a sliver of land owned by a neighbor which was maybe 50 to 75 yards wide. Just beyond that is the Ocala National Forest. You could do all the public land fishing and hunting you could ever want without being more than mere minutes from your home. As Leon and Vicky gave us a tour all I could think was, how they retired the right way. I could only dream to have something like this one day.

Now, before I continue, I think it is important to address trophies and hunting. Without speaking in absolutes or generalizations, in the US, it is illegal

Chapter 2: An Intro to a New Hunter

to hunt an animal for just a trophy. The only exception are invasive species which are causing a negative impact to the ecosystem, and even then there are exceptions to that exception. Hunting rules and regulations are about as clear as mud usually, so make sure you research the rules for your area. These laws are usually called wanton waste laws, and in a nutshell, it outlaws the wanton and willful waste of wildlife. What this means is you must harvest the animal you hunt and use the meat from that harvest. It is also illegal to sell the meat, so you can give the meat away or eat it, but you cannot throw it away. So, when most people talk about "trophy hunters" they are often referring to poachers which are very different, and do not abide by or enter the conversation of ethics and conservation that a hunter does. If I were in a position that I could only take either the trophy of my quarry, or the meat, I would choose the meat every time. The fact that I can take both is a bonus.

I say all that to say this, what was as impressive as Leon's property was the incredible collection of trophies he had collected over his life as a hunter. As we walked in, we were greeted first with his Turkey grand slam birds. He had one of every sub species of turkey found in the US. As you continue to enter you can see different waterfowl, all kinds of big game from around the world such as a Tahr, Red Stag, White Tail Deer, a Black Bear, African Warthog, and Coyotes. Each of these trophies were snapshots to adventures Leon had been on throughout his life. They each had their own story, experiences, and memories.

As I am admiring the amazing collection Leon emerges from a back room. He is a little older than Uncle Manny, on the shorter side, very skinny and had salt and pepper hair. It had a bit more salt than pepper. His personality and heart though, could fill the length and width of his property. He came out with a huge smile and a ton of energy. He was like a car ready for a drag race, revving to go and waiting for the green light.

He and Vicky had prepared a full breakfast for us. We ate and drank coffee in a dinette that overlooked the lake. At my insistence, Leon regaled us with some of his favorite hunting stories and pointed out the a few of members of his collection as he told the story of their specific hunts. He has hunted in Africa, New Zealand and across the US. I mean I don't know how he didn't have his own TV show with how much he knew about hunting not just one type of game, but so many. and all of his experiences were more incredible than the last.

He recalled one of his favorite hunts was for an Antelope in Africa where he stayed with locals in a tiny village. Once successful in his hunt, the guide that had been showing him around had prepared a traditional African meal with the meat from his quarry. The rest of the meat was donated to the Village, as is customary for those type of hunts, and

He brought home the cape to be mounted in remembrance of the trip. As he reminisced, he was more detailed about his experience in the village and the cuisine and how friendly and hospitable they all were than about the hunt itself. I found it interesting that while the main goal of hunting is to of course harvest an animal, what is remembered most is not the harvest itself, but everything leading up it.

During breakfast I kind of had an informal interview of the first two hunters I had ever met and volleyed question after question. In hindsight, it must have been not all that much different than when my son asks me question after question over any topic that pops up in his head while sitting in the backseat on our way to, well... anywhere. I must have seemed like a child on the first day of school to them.

What really got me excited about the coming hunt was his answer to my favorite question for a

Chapter 2: An Intro to a New Hunter

hunter, especially a hunter with this much experience with different species of game. I asked him if he could only eat one game meat for the rest of his life and never have any other type of meat again, what would it be. His answer? Wild Hog! Uncle Manny was in agreeance as well. I was stoked! If we were successful today, I would be bringing home some high-quality game for my family.

Chapter 3: Bringin' Home the Bacon

B y the time we got done with breakfast and my newbie hunter interview of both Leon and Uncle Manny, it was time for us to get ready and go. My sister in law worked at Bass Pro at the time so she got me my first camo. I didn't know if it was necessary or not as we were hunting from tree stands that day, but I was wearing it with pride anyway. We arrived at the outfitter's property right as the property manager and our guide for the day were opening the gate. We pulled

Chapter 3: Bringin' Home the Bacon

in and started grabbing our daypacks and our rifles. I was borrowing Uncle Manny's .300 blackout AR; I still love that Rifle. Uncle Manny had taken me to the range almost weekly leading up to this hunt, just so I could get comfortable with the rifle and set me up to take the best shot possible. The guide and manager went over the ground rules and told us we would be driven to three different parts of the property so we would have a better opportunity at being successful. Uncle Manny and I would be in our own stands, and Leon would be hunting from a blind near a small pond with his wife spectating.

We piled into a UTV and take off down a trail through the trees and palmetto bushes. As we turn our first corner a medium sized hog and 2 smaller hogs dart across the trail. This is a great sign. I immediately get that giddy feeling in my stomach. After a minute or two we arrive at the first stand. This is my stop and our guide walks me through the trees and the bushes.

About 100 yards into the brush there is a clearing with a feeder and off to the left is the stand. I tie a rope to my day bag and rifle and climb up to the seat. I start hauling them up after me. No sooner than untying them and getting situated do I see a sounder headed my way made up of a huge sow, a medium sized boar with 2 other medium sized sows and a piglet. I couldn't believe my luck. My first reaction is to get a few pictures of them before I remembered the purpose of this trip. I could see my target as I raise the AR to my shoulder. The largest Sow was tan with dark spots and looked like she had a good amount of fat on her. I quietly rest my rifle on the guardrail of the tree stand. I raise the scope to my eye, keeping in mind the eye relief and put her right in my crosshairs. I progress through the mental checklist I had developed while training with Uncle Manny. I steady my breathing, I am going to squeeze not pull the trigger, I am going to do so in the pause between breaths and not hold my breath, the shot should surprise me. As I do so, I think to myself, do I really want this to be it? Do I want to have it end so fast? I pull this trigger right now and my first hunt is over within minutes of it even beginning. I decided to not take the shot. It felt too easy. I mean I saw 3 hogs on the way in from the UTV and here I have 5 more within minutes of sitting down. I lower the rifle and I let them walk off into the brush.

As they lumber off the area seems to get quiet again as my excitement from the encounter starts to wear off. I sit in the stand quietly donating blood to bird sized mosquitos waiting for my next opportunity. After 15 minutes that feel like an eternity, I am kicking myself. If I were to tell Uncle Manny, I saw 5 Hogs, had a clear shot, and I didn't take it because I didn't want it to end, I think he would make me walk back to Miami. To make matters worse, after an hour of sitting there regretting my decision, I can hear pigs rolling around in some mud puddle behind some bushes to my back left, but I couldn't see them. Almost as if they were taunting me.

I continue to sit and wait. And sit. and wait some more. I can hear some rustling to my 7 o'clock. I look over my shoulder and I see a spotted hog. I couldn't get into shooting position without spooking it, but I was able to snap a quick picture. He was a little smaller than I would have wanted but at this point I was not going to let another shot slip by. I think to myself, "Had he been in a better position, I would have taken the shot." He turns away from me and disappears into the bushes in the direction of those other hogs that were splashing in the puddle earlier.

What feels like a lifetime again passes and I can see what looks like the same group of hogs from earlier making their way back. I get as excited as a calf on a teat! They're making a beeline right back to the feeder! I get the big girl in my sights again. She is marching in steadily when suddenly, she stops and starts smelling the air. CRAP! She is catching my scent! I know it. I can feel the wind at the back of my neck. It is now or never. I aim at her head because I didn't have a clean shot at her heart or lungs. Just like I practiced with Uncle Manny at the range. I steady my breathing and slowly squeeze the trigger so that the shot surprises me. Nothing.

Rookie lesson number 1: *When you are ready to take a shot. Chamber a damn round.*

Surprisingly the sow isn't moving. She is cautiously smelling the air and looking around. She isn't coming any closer, but she isn't running off either. I try to chamber my round slowly like you would on a bolt action. I pull the action back, let the round come up and out of the magazine and into the chamber. I then slowly let the action go back into place. I put her in my crosshairs and slowly squeeze the trigger again... CLICK. It misfired. Well not misfired, but it wasn't chambered correctly because the round wasn't seated correctly.

Rookie lesson number 2: *You can't slowly and quietly chamber a round like you would on a bolt action for an AR. You need to pull the action back and let it do its job.*

The click I just heard was louder than any round I would have fired. At least to my ears it was. I realize what I did wrong. I pull the action back catching the ejecting round and I let the action go successfully chambering a round now. That sound though, was enough to cost me my second chance at that sow. The sound of the action, paired with my scent she was definitely picking up, was enough for her to turn on her hooves and high tail it out of there. I felt like the biggest loser on the face of the earth. Not only had I decided not to shoot on my first opportunity I missed my second opportunity because I didn't think to chamber a damn round when I got into the stand. I was in shock and was just totally down on myself.

Chapter 3: Bringin' Home the Bacon

I sat there distraught just staring at the .300 blackout round in my hand in utter disbelief. How in the hell was I going to tell the two seasoned hunters that came on this trip for my sake, that I missed two opportunities?

I prayed hard at that point for one more opportunity. I couldn't go home empty handed. In my mind this would be a total failure if I went home empty handed at this point. I had made a deal with myself before the trip to not get upset if I didn't come home with meat for my freezer as this was hunting not your leisurely stroll down the butcher aisle at your local grocer. I knew it was a possibility. But I could never have prepared myself mentally for two missed opportunities. It never occurred to me at all. I thought of it as a binary situation, if I see hogs, it meant meat for my freezer. If I didn't, then it meant an unsuccessful hunt. I never thought I would see them and not be able to get a shot off. That scenario never played in my head.

As I am sitting there, sulking for the next hour or so, I here rustling below me. A Boar pops its head out of a bush. He is almost directly below me, so I didn't want to reach for my rifle and spook him. He was looking directly at the feeder and scanning the area around it. I can quietly reach on the seat next to me for my phone and snap a picture. As I do so, he slowly walks over to the feeder and discovers some corn that had been knocked on the ground by some squirrels earlier in the day. He is about 70 or so yards from me, but he is facing totally away from me, so I don't really have a shot at any vitals. My round is chambered, and my crosshairs are right on him. I had heard about something called the Texas heart shot which flashed through my head. Basically, you aim for the animal's anus as a bullseye and the round is supposed to make it straight to the heart. That wasn't the type of shooting I was interested in taking, nor did it sound too appetizing for the meat I would harvest. Also, it kind of felt like something put on forums but not a

Chapter 3: Bringin' Home the Bacon

shot anyone had ever really took, so while I briefly considered it, I erred on the side of caution.

I just wait patiently for a good shot. As much as I tell myself to control my breathing, I am sucking wind like if I just ran 5 miles. My breath was heavy with the disappointment of my earlier bad decisions, and the knowledge that this would likely be my last opportunity.

He finishes up the corn and turns a full 180 as he prepares to walk directly back where he came from. Directly back to the bushes that were just below me. He is now facing me head on and as he takes a few steps he notices one last piece of corn on the ground. He cranes his neck down, and in my head, I can hear my inner voice scream "NOW! Now's my shot!" I squeeze that trigger and the round hits him dead center on the back of his neck. He stiffens and immediately drops. Once he does, he begins to convulse violently. I think he is suffering not factoring in that the round completely severed his spine at the neck, my reaction was to take two more shots at his now exposed chest to where his heart would be.

Once he stops convulsing my whole body begins to shake uncontrollably. I almost feel like I couldn't breathe and could only manage a shaky and repeated, "Oh my god" still in a whisper. I couldn't believe I HAD DONE IT! After two missed opportunities on a 1-day hunt, I was able to still come home with some meat. I needed a little more than a minute to gather myself and stop my nerves from shaking my whole body. I tie up my rifle and bag again and lower it to the ground and start my climb down. As soon as my feet crunch the leaves at the foot of the ladder, my guide emerges from the bushes.

"Congrats! That's a damn good shot there!" he excitedly whispered to me. He then snapped my first ever grip and grin picture with my first ever wild boar on my first ever hunt. We dragged him back to

Chapter 3: Bringin' Home the Bacon

the UTV and drove back to camp. Uncle Manny and Leon were still out there and hadn't taken a shot yet. The guide hung the boar up on a game hanger and I asked him if I could clean the hog since it was my first hog. Not only did he say yes, but he taught me what is still the fastest way I have ever seen to clean large game.

At the end of the day Uncle Manny got a shot at a decent size sow as well and Leon got a shot opportunity but was just a little bit high on his shot placement. It was a clean miss, which if you miss, you will always prefer it to be a clean miss. No hunter wants to hit an animal where it injures them but doesn't drop them having them go through unnecessary suffering.

We cleaned and iced the meat and unplugged the cooler to allow the moisture to drain. "You want the meat cold, not wet." Uncle Manny explains tome as he loads the cooler back onto the back of his truck, doing his best to incline it in a way that allows the water to escape. We wrapped it up by grabbing a quick bite at a local diner we had seen on the way in and went back to Leon's homestead.

Chapter 4: Rounding Out the First Hunt

We still had two days on our trip and Leon and his wife really went out of their way to make sure we had a great time. Leon started off the next morning with some skeet shooting which I had never done before either. I wasn't hitting anything when we started, and as Leon taught me the basics of leading the target and proper stance, by the end of it I was hitting a minimum of 2 out of 3 targets. Leon said he was determined to make a waterfowl hunter out of me as well, now that he knew I liked hunting. He said Duck was his second favorite game meat, which of course, got me thinking.

For lunch we headed to their local community center where he and his wife volunteer time in the kitchen to cook for others in the area, including visitors to the nearby K.O.A. campground. The money earned helped feed others less fortunate and fund community projects.

It was an older building with a gravel parking lot. Once you walked in it was a large rectangular space that was totally open with the only internal wall being the one that separated the kitchen from the dining area. Everyone there was incredibly friendly, and it was evident that Vicky and Leon are very well liked in the community. While at the community center we met some nice folks that were staying at the nearby campground. We found out that they had all gone fishing for prawns, and they had gotten tired of cleaning them and said they

Chapter 4: Rounding Out the First Hunt

would give us what they had left over. Little did we know, we would be gifted a large cooler full of them. We spent a few hours of the early afternoon cleaning them and preparing a hefty amount for dinner. Leon said he and Vicky would be making their homemade alfredo sauce, so it was shrimp alfredo on the menu that night.

In the late afternoon, before dinner, we had finished cleaning the entire batch, and so he took us out on his pontoon boat for a few hours to tour the lake and we also did a little bit of freshwater fishing. The lake was incredible. There was no wind which gave the water this plate glass look that had no ripples or movement other than the occasional alligator or turtle breaking the surface. It reflected the sky like a giant mirror.

Before the Rodman Dam was built, the land was never cleared, so while this makes navigating the lake a little bit more hazardous, it provides an incredible number of underwater features for all kinds of fish which in turn brings all kinds of wildlife. It also makes for incredible landscapes as you have cypress and pine trees that appear to be growing from the lake bottom and adorned with Spanish moss draping from branch to branch like garland on a Christmas tree.

One of my most memorable sights was of an American bald eagle perched atop a cypress in the middle of the lake watching the surrounding area like a sentry manning a post. This was the first wild bald eagle I had ever seen and is one of my favorite animals in North America. Whenever I see one, I usually make it a point to stop and admire them for as long as possible. There are about 150,000 currently so if you think about it, it is less likely you see one of these than a whitetail deer (32 million in North America). These guys though had a rough go in the early 20th Century. Once estimated to have numbered in the 300,000 to 400,000 range, there was a pesticide used in the 20th century that caused an issue with males becoming sterile, and

Chapter 4: Rounding Out the First Hunt

issues with how they metabolized calcium so females would lay thinner eggs that couldn't support the weight of a brooding mother. Their numbers dwindled until there were only 412 nesting pairs in the 48 contiguous states. Thanks to conservation efforts their numbers have steadily climbed, and they were removed from the list of endangered and threatened species in 2007. There is also something to be said of the feeling one gets while hunting and sitting in the woods or in this case fishing on a lake and seeing the symbol of our great nation hunting and fishing just the same.

This was absolutely one of the most treasured experiences I have ever had and both Leon and Uncle Manny really went out of their way to not only bring in a new hunter into the community but make my first hunt something I would never forget. If there was any lingering doubt that I was now a newly minted proud hunter, it was all gone a week later when Uncle Manny made me his world-famous Wild Boar Meatloaf. Nothing has ever tasted better.

Chapter 5: High Fence Harvest

After my first hunt I really started to take an interest in learning more about the sport/hobby and just about nature in general. I have come to realize that while most people think of hunting as one general term to describe one activity, it's a broad term that lumps in a community with many different methods and sub communities. There are many different types of hunting and I'm not even just talking the type of weapon used such as archery vs. muzzleloader vs. rifle. That is still too broad. With each one of those weapons you still have different types of hunting you can do with those. I have only ever experienced rifle hunting even then I have not quite done it all. You have hunting over bait, tree stand hunting, hunting from a blind, hunting from the ground without a blind, spot and stalk and the list goes on. Each of these have their own intricacies and details to be learned.

Throughout the year after my first hunt I learned about tactics, the importance of practicing with the rifle and exact round you intend to hunt with, and how to think about things like scent and topography of the area you are hunting. I really got hooked on a show called MeatEater, for any of those readers who may be new to hunting, you should really check it out if you haven't yet. This show really started to get me excited about hunting public land. I thought about how much more challenging it would be and in turn how much more rewarding a successful hunt would be. One of the many draws for me was the concept of preparing meals for my

Chapter 5: High Fence Harvest

family and friends that I had a hand in from the absolute beginning to the absolute end. It was that endeavor that had me try to use herbs and vegetables I grow in my garden in the dish as well and only use store bought items for those that I couldn't grow myself because of space or just geography.

While I was fantasizing about a public land hunt, I was invited for a group hog hunt on a private property with an outfitter near Lake Okeechobee. I of course emphatically said yes. I kept my expectations of harvesting a hog myself low considering there was a decent sized group going and it was my brother's first hunt. I went mostly to support him and be there for his first ever hog, so while I would be hunting, I wasn't dead set on bringing meat home myself. I wanted him to.

It wasn't very far from my home in Northwest Palm Beach County, maybe about 2 hours away. We got there about 8 am and met up with our group. The rest of the group included Uncle Manny's brother, and a few others that worked with Uncle Manny and had actually been the ones who found the place.

The entrance to the property was overgrown with towering sawgrass and thick palmettos. It had a metal ranch style gate that was about twelve feet wide. The surrounding area was all ranches and farmland. There were no clear markings on the gate itself, so we drove past it a few times before finally realizing that was the entrance. There were 2 guides that showed up on the other side in a small 2-seater UTV, they unlocked the gate and swung it open for us to drive into the ranch and toward the ranch house.

The house was more of a mobile home that had a large porch attached to it. If you were sitting on the porch looking outward, you would see a large pond to your left surrounded by shrubs. In the middle of the pond was a juvenile alligator. I am no

Chapter 5: High Fence Harvest

alligator expert, so I don't know exactly what size an alligator is when it leaves momma, so I made a mental note to avoid the pond just in case.

***

I love alligators and find them interesting. As any good old Floridian should. I also respect them a whole lot. Although, alligators don't generally attack humans or anything large enough to fight back or that they can't swallow in one gulp. They are patient, yet lazy hunters and have been known to stalk their prey for hours before attacking. If their prey does fight back in any significant way, it is usually abandoned. Generally, attacks in Florida are defensive in nature and are quite rare. There were only 12 alligator attacks in 2017 and only a total of 498 since Florida Fish and Wildlife started keeping track in 1948. Those are low numbers considering there are an estimated 1.25 million Alligators in the state as of 2018. Even with those numbers being so high, according to the Florida

Fish and Wildlife Commission, they are listed as a "species of special concern" in Florida and as "threatened" federally because of their similar appearance to the endangered American crocodile. A little-known fact, there are an estimated 1,000 crocodiles living in FL as well.

***

For this hunt, I had packed a daypack with a snack, some water, my thermacel and a shemagh (large lightweight scarf used to wrap one's head and or face in a warm or hot climate) to keep the mosquitoes off my face. We got off the truck, grabbed our gear and our rifles, and we were led to a swamp buggy. If you haven't seen one, it is a common sight in rural FL, heck even in some areas that are not so rural. They really look like a pontoon boat with monster truck tires underneath them and a large exposed engine. The wide tread of the tires allows for grip in the soft, wet, and often muddy ground that is common throughout the state. I assumed we were going to be taken to a tree stand or blind somewhere on the property and each of us would be hunting alone. It turns out that was not the case. We were informed that we would be driving around on the swamp buggy trying to track down the hogs.

I started to realize that this was a little different than what I thought it was once they said that. I had a feeling I wouldn't be needing my daypack after all. The property was a working cattle ranch. We were advised that we needed to be sure of our shot and any accidental injury or death of one of their cattle meant we would need to purchase that cow. Their fee was several thousand dollars. If that doesn't make you be extra certain of your target and what lies beyond it, I don't know what will.

We drove around the ranch and saw a good amount of cattle, but no hog. After about 20 to 30 minutes of driving around we arrive at yet, another gate, which took us into another piece of the property where there weren't any cattle in sight. Hogs in Florida generally like to hide in the clumps and groves of saw palmettos. Their thick hide isn't really disturbed by the plants saw-like stem, and it helps keep them cool in the humid Florida weather. It also helps them hide from predators, such as the Florida panther and black bears.

In this new section of the property, we drove from palmetto grove to palmetto grove and all of a sudden, we began finding groups of hogs after groups of hogs. One by one each of our group got a hog. As I started to see how successful this hunt was turning out to be given our number, I really started to get this feeling that this wasn't a hunt but a culling. I was the last to have an opportunity at a shot and there wasn't a hog in sight except for a little piglet no older than a month or two. I wasn't interested in hunting a piglet so I told them I would pass it up.

Chapter 5: High Fence Harvest

After about 30 to 40 minutes of driving around without another hog in sight, one of the guides says he needed to take care of something in the office and left. The second guide took the steering wheel to continue driving us around to look for a hog. After only 5 minutes since the disappearance of the first guide, one large sow and 2 juvenile hogs sprint across the field about 200 hundred yards from us. I am overtaken by the emotion of seeing a worthy hog I rest my rifle on the guardrail and zoom in and focus my scope as the guide tries to get me closer.

We close the distance to approximately 100 yards and the hog starts to sprint again. I lead her by three notches on my crosshair and squeeze the trigger. She immediately drops, rolls, and slides for another few feet because of the momentum. As we drive closer, we notice I had shot her in the spine, so she was paralyzed but not quite gone. My heart sunk. I quickly took another shot at her head to end her suffering and that was it.

The excitement was nowhere what it was when I had my first hunt. It felt off and while I did hit my moving target from a moving platform, I don't ever recommend that type of shooting, and would never take that shot again. Sure, it was one of the best shots I have ever taken and was testament to the time put in at the range and the training I had received from Uncle Manny, and significant amount of luck as well. However, it wasn't an ethical shot. I got lucky in paralyzing the hog and ending her suffering quickly, but in another scenario, I could have just as easily injured the animal and caused it needless suffering and never found it.

As the haze of emotion started to wear off, we all started to realize something. This wasn't a real hunt. I don't mean the fact that we hunted down the hogs from the swamp buggy, it's not my favorite way to hunt, but perfectly legal for this animal and I can see the draw it would have in Florida. What had me feeling off was something else. As I looked around the ranch on our way back, I realized that

Chapter 5: High Fence Harvest

this outfitter had penned up their hogs in a mock hunt. We were driven around the working ranch for a while under the guise of hog hunting, but there wasn't a hog in sight. Then we were taken to a separate fenced off area where we easily found hogs for everyone in the party except, me as the last shooter. After some time, one guide disappears, and we miraculously find one just minutes after his departure? I was not happy at all. I mean sure I got some meat for my freezer and I don't want to take a dig on any kind of hunting, but this just wasn't for me. I can see how this would appeal to maybe a first-time hunter for a guaranteed hog or to someone who would have difficulty stomping around the woods, but it just didn't jive with my idea of what hunting meant for me.

Rookie lesson number 3: be wary of outfitters with a 100% guaranteed hunt and don't be afraid of asking if it is a high fence hunt.

This experience solidified it for me. I was done with outfitters for the time being and I wanted my next hunt to be a DIY public lands hunt.

Chapter 6: Public Land Buck

Chapter 6: Public Land Buck

After I got back from that hunt my research into public land hunting had shifted into high gear. I binge watched all the MeatEater episodes on Netflix more than once. I then learned the host of the show, Steven Rinella, also had 2 books published. Both are incredible books, but my favorite is his book *Meat Eater Adventures from the Life of an American Hunter*. He chronicles his life growing up as a hunter and his time as a trapper in the Midwest in a really descriptive and easy to read way that captured me from page 1. I had contracted the Public Lands bug bad. I was enamored with the challenge it presented and could only imagine how rewarding it must be if you are successful on a completely DIY public lands hunt.

The only problem is everything I read about public land hunting seemed to point to western hunting. There are a ton of resources out there about hunting big game in places like Alaska, Colorado, Montana, and Wyoming. Those are definitely some bucket list hunts for me but not feasible for my first ever public land hunt. I started to research refuges, wildlife management areas and national forests closer to home.

In Florida the two that seem to be the most popular are Big Cypress National Preserve which is basically the everglades and is just north of Everglades National Park. The second was Ocala National Forest in Central Florida.

Chapter 6: Public Land Buck

In the state of Florida, the only tags issued for deer are for does. You are able to hunt bucks throughout the state as long as it meets the state guidelines and the guidelines of the area you are hunting. Some areas have stricter guidelines than the state, so it is always important to check what they are. What Florida does have is something called Quota Permits and Special Opportunity Permits. You basically put your name into a lotto with hundreds to thousands of other hunters that may have put in for the same area. You choose five areas you are interested in and if you win in say 2 of those, it will draw for you the property you had highest on your list of choices. If you don't win any you have the opportunity to try again in another phase. There are 3 phases each year. This is a very quick and over the top review of the process as it is only for the state of Florida. It gets much more complicated especially in the westernmost states, and can be very different from state to state. How to draw hunting tags could really be its own book.

I put in for several areas but the area I really wanted to hunt was Big Cypress National Preserve. I read that hunting Big Cypress was one of the more challenging hunts in Florida, at least for deer. Not because game wasn't abundant, but because of the hunting pressure in previous years. The pressure had gotten so bad that it is the one place where hogs have been all but eradicated in the state. Also, the bucks in South Florida don't really grow as large nor do they have the biggest antlers. For me though, I didn't care about that. After my disappointment with that High fence hunt, I wanted the challenge, I didn't care about the size of the antlers.

I put in my request and it took about 8 weeks to hear back. I had placed Big Cypress as my number one option and had won the quota permit for the Bear Island Unit of the preserve. The permit allowed me to take 1 guest, so of course I called my mentor, Uncle Manny, first and asked him if he

Chapter 6: Public Land Buck

would be interested in a DIY public land hunt. HE WAS IN! not only was he in, it would be his first public land hunt as well. He had always hunted on private leases and with outfitters in the past. He had also been disappointed with the last hunt we had and was excited for something new.

I later learned that it was a high probability draw for that unit because most hunters had long given up on the area and moved further up state. It was considered one of the most challenging hunts in my home state. That would sound daunting or discouraging to most people, but I was stoked! I could not wait, and I started to count down the days to our trip much like a kid counts down to Christmas.

The weeks leading up to the hunt included many screenshots and pictures back and forth of gear we had bought, were buying, or wanted to buy. These messages were highly confidential because we knew our wives would be hunting us if they ever found out.

Chapter 7: Public Land Buck Day 1

The Big Cypress Preserve is 729,000 acres that borders the Everglades National Park to its south and is sandwiched between the Everglades & Francis S. Taylor Wildlife Management Area and the Florida Panther Wildlife Refuge. To put its size into perspective, it is larger than the entire state of Rhode Island. It is also the nation's first ever national preserve. It makes up a large portion of the state's largest contiguous habitat for the Florida Panther.

***

Once plentiful, the Florida Panther was found throughout not just the entire state but throughout the gulf coast all the way to Louisiana. Unfortunately, it is now mostly limited to the south western part of Florida. Their numbers are estimated to be in the area of 120 to 130. The most optimistic projections are estimating no more than 250. This low number has raised concerns about genetic diversity and makes them vulnerable to just about every threat.

They naturally have a large range where males have a territory that spans 200 square miles and females between 70 to 80. This is a challenge in getting their population to bounce back especially since attempts at reintroducing them in other areas have been met with fear.

Chapter 7: Public Land Buck Day 1

They are a subspecies of the more commonly known, mountain lion, and is the only sub species that remains in the eastern U.S. today.

***

The day before the hunt I drove the hour and a half down to Uncle Manny's house in Miami so we could get an early start on our scout day and to be able to set up camp comfortably during the daylight hours. The drive there was uneventful. It's about 2 hours away from his house and after about 30 minutes you pass the last large building you see which is the Miccosukee Resort and Gaming Casino.

It is managed by the Miccosukee tribe which has an incredible history. They were once part of the Creek Nation which originally held the territory that now makes up Alabama, Northern Florida, parts of Georgia and southern Tennessee. The Miccosukee tribe migrated to Florida before it was a part of the newly minted United States. During the 1800s, like many other tribes, most of them were moved out west. About 100 tribesmen however, eluded capture and remained in the Everglades. It wasn't until 1962, about 3 years after Buffalo Tiger had gotten international recognition for the Miccosukee as a sovereign nation within the United States, that the U.S. Secretary of the Interior approved the Miccosukee constitution and the tribe was officially recognized.

Once you pass the casino there is nothing but Lillie pads and sawgrass on either side of the two-lane road with an alligator or two sprinkled in. Occasionally, you may pass a shack offering airboat rides. The road itself is commonly known as alligator alley and be sure you fill up on gas, because you won't hit another station until you are near the opposite side of the Florida peninsula.

Chapter 7: Public Land Buck Day 1

The last leg of the drive in is a long and dusty dirt road that crosses under Interstate 75 a few miles before you arrive at the Bear Island unit. As we pull in, we stop at the game warden's hut to check in. It was a small wooden shack that looks like it has been there forever, but not really sure how it had survived the recent hurricanes that had blown through the area. It was slightly larger than the average garden shed and sat on top of a concrete slab. To the right of the shed is a gate to a gnarly looking road that requires an off-road permit from the Fish and Wildlife Commission for entry. To the right of that is an information board under a small wooden roof with a deer hanger attached to the side and a small lockbox that is used so you can pay the nightly fee if you are planning on camping out.

I have noticed that some people can be really weary or fearful of game wardens and most cases they are people who would have no reason to be. I really don't have a clue why that is the case. I have learned that they tend to be a fountain of information. Many hunt the same area so they may not give you specific hunting spots of course, but you can glean some pretty good tips from them. Places to pay special attention to or places to stay away from. In this case our game warden was an older man very tall and skinny with a thick southern accent. He has hunted the Big Cypress for most of his life and was able to tell us that while our quota permit allowed for Hog, it was likely that we wouldn't see one. Between hunters, alligators, panthers and bears, there aren't many left in the area. Deer, he said, were plentiful. They were, however, skittish and weary, so could be a challenge to find them.

Our game warden went over the rules of the unit and went over what size buck is allowed for harvest. In this case we were allowed to hunt a buck only and he needed a minimum of 2 points on one side of an inch or longer. Basically, a forkie (buck with forked antlers) and up, no spikes, button bucks (buck who has only grown a nub of an antler that is too short to call a spike) or does.

We filled out our check in paperwork, paid for the campsite rental, and drove on to find an open tent site. After looking at the trails we would be walking we opted for a tent site near the end of the camp area and close to a walk-in only trail that led to the northeast area of the preserve.

The site has a trimmed lawn that is U shaped. On the curve of each side of the U there was a small stretch that went further back where you could put a tent. It looked almost like the shape of the Greek letter mu (μ). We pulled the truck into the middle of the U and offloaded. There was a picnic table directly behind the truck and a small fire pit slightly off to the right and diagonal from the table. About 50 feet from the picnic table was a small brush line that had what looked to be newly growing saw palmettos. Beyond that was a giant slough surrounded by brush and pine trees on the opposite side.

We unloaded and set up camp. The tent was up against the brush line and to its left was a sitting area we set up and shaded it with an old gazebo cover Uncle Manny had in his garage. We then found some dry wood throughout the camp site and piled it up for a fire later that evening. Once satisfied with camp we excitedly grabbed our rifles and orange vests and set off scouting.

The entrance to the walk-in only path was about 300 yards from our camp. There was a rusted old gate that was locked. It forced you to veer off to a small footpath to the left of the gate. As soon as you make it to the other side there is a large puddle that spans the width of the path and then some. It looked too deep to cross without getting unnecessarily and uncomfortably soggy, so we opted to walk through a muddy area off to the right

Chapter 7: Public Land Buck Day 1

through some tall cypress, Brazilian pepper bushes, and saw palmettos.

Once we make it to the other side you walk another 10 feet or so and you hit a giant clearing with pines, sawgrass, palmettos, and palm trees lining either side of the path. We took a minute here just taking in the vastness and wildness of the landscape. It is astonishing how you feel like you are in a whole other world after just a short drive. No traffic, cell phones, or even people. Just a light breeze gently pushing the sawgrass in a hypnotizing sway and rustling the leaves.

After spending a quick moment taking this in, we walk to the right of this clearing and notice a small slough with plenty of bushes for cover. This looked like a good place for a sit. It being so close to camp though we decided to note this place as a potential hunting location with a good watering hole and we kept walking down the path. We got about a mile in before we noticed the first sign of deer in the area.

There were several rubs where you could clearly tell a buck had rubbed his antlers on low hanging branches. It looked like it was all concentrated to the area on the right side of the path.

To the left was some very thick saw palmettos that did not look like a pleasant walk for us or any animal taller than a hog. We veered off the path to follow the deer sign and noticed an old rusted tree stand that someone had left in the field.

Rookie lesson number 4: Don't be that guy. If you set up a tree stand on public property, be sure to take it back out, besides if you don't want it, I am pretty sure there are plenty of other hunters who wouldn't mind taking it off of your hands.

We took it as a good sign that this was a decent place to hunt. Obviously, someone else had thought so as well. Next to the tree stand was a decent sized pond surrounded by a tree line of pine trees and palmettos. There were some egrets, herons and noisy ducks in the pond. Location 2, dubbed the rusty tree stand, looked better than location 1. I marked it on my GPS, and we headed back to the path. We walked another quarter mile before Uncle Manny spotted a hunter in a tree stand ahead and a little to the left of the path. We didn't want to blow out any deer he may have been hunting so we backed out slowly and decided to go back to the rusty tree stand and just hunt there the rest of the afternoon.

Rookie lesson number 5: *Don't set your tree stand up near a path on public land. Not everyone may be so considerate in backing away and you are blocking the path for other hunters to continue to a spot deeper into the woods.*

The afternoon was uneventful. We sat on the ground up against a pine tree and we were obscured by some palmettos. Wind was in our face and we spent the afternoon glassing the opposite tree line on the other side of the pond.

We got right up to last shooting light before we called it quits and started the mile or so walk back to camp. Now, I am a city boy who happens to love the country and the outdoors. I was not used to the outdoors as much as I thought I was though and didn't register how dark it gets and how fast it gets that damn dark. I am not going to lie, there was a good amount of apprehension walking in the progressing blackness and more than a thought or two of bears and alligators on my mind. Of course, this was not verbalized at all to Uncle Manny who I am pretty sure only had dinner on his mind. He walked through the woods like it was his back yard.

Once back at camp I started the fire and whipped out the aluminum foil. We were going to make hunter's pie. Most people call it hobo pie, but my son called it hunter's pie since he had first seen it on a hunting show I was watching, and it just stuck.

Basically, you season some ground beef anyway you like and add any kind of root vegetables. You seal it up in an aluminum foil pouch and then toss it in the fire to cook.

Rookie lesson number 6: If you plan to cook over an open fire some hunter's pie. Make sure to bring some long metal tongs or other utensil. It's not fun fishing it out with sticks and bare hands.

Neither of us had thought to bring tongs so we used sticks and our knives to coax the sizzling tin pockets out of the fire and onto some plates. We open up our silver protein and veggie packages and let the steam waft away some of the mosquitos for a few seconds. The meal isn't the prettiest of plating, but it tasted incredible. After eating we called it a night.

This being the first night I had ever spent out in the swamp, it was incredible to notice how loud the quiet can be. As I lay there on my air mattress with nothing more than a thin piece of fabric sheltering me from the outside world, I take notice there were no sounds of cars, neighbors, horns, or sirens. No distant hums of music from a party in the neighborhood, no car alarms, or any of the other of the many sound effects and soundtracks one becomes accustomed to in the city. After laying down I first notice the incredible quiet. So peaceful and complementary to the surrounding darkness now that there was no campfire or headlamp lighting the surrounding area. Then, amazingly, the sounds of the night slowly become louder and clearer. The rustling of branches in the light breeze, cracking twigs under the weight of even something as small as a raccoon, and the calls of frogs, crickets, and other nocturnal neighbors. I close my eyes and drift away with relative ease. But something in my reptilian brain kept me waking every 30 to 40 minutes to take stock of my surroundings before drifting off again. It reminded me of deer that bed down but seem to pop their head up and scan the area before lowering their head and dozing off again. It is incredible that no matter how much we have advanced as a species, there are still some animalistic instincts that are present. Like the, instinct to remain alert even while sleeping to avoid becoming prey. You know that once you are out in the wilderness, be that a swamp or a forest, you are no longer the undisputed top of the food chain. All the statistics in the world about how unlikely it is to be attacked by a bear, or an alligator, or a panther makes no difference to your subconscious and you remain alert, even while you sleep.

Chapter 8: Public Land Buck
Day 2

We woke up the next morning at about 4:30 AM. We threw on our camo, blaze orange vests and boots. I wake up feeling fairly well rested, but I am a coffee freak and will drink hot coffee even if it is 102 degrees out. So, I started to fiddle with my camp stove and try to make us some. After about 5 minutes of fumbling with my pack, and coffee gear, and trying to get the stove set up, Uncle Manny tosses me an iced coffee from the cooler and says,

Chapter 8: Public Land Buck Day 2

"put that crap away, let's get out there." Realizing that this was a faster way to get the caffeine in my system and it was cold which would help with the hot humid morning, I toss the camp stove back in the truck and we head out.

After walking through the dark once without issue, married with the fact that I was not 100% awake just yet, this walk wasn't as nerve wracking for me. We walk quietly under the glow of our red headlamps, careful not to slip on the ground that is slightly muddier and slicker than yesterday thanks to the morning dew. The walk was uneventful, that is until about halfway to the rusty tree stand, there is this incredibly loud fluttering and the sound of a tree branch snapping back into place after a weight just left it. My soul felt like it exited my body and I must have convulsed 3 times before I reflexively reached for my pistol on my belt but didn't draw.

After a few seconds that felt like an eternity, I realized it was a damn turkey buzzard that had been scared by my groggy and sloppy stomps which bumped it from its roost. As soon as I realized that, all I hear from behind me is a deep chuckle from Uncle Manny. No words. No witty quip. Just a chuckle that said all he needed to say. I wouldn't be living this one down any time soon.

The rest of the day was quiet. We got totally skunked. No sign of deer at the rusty tree stand or the area around it. The most excitement we got was sometime near the middle of the afternoon another hunter noisily walked right behind us and never noticed we were there.

When you are sitting quietly your mind tends to wander. You start thinking about the most off the wall and irrational things. While on the sit, I got to thinking, was I good enough with my .308 to shoot one of the ducks from this distance just to bring some meat back to camp? It would have to be a head shot of course, otherwise there wouldn't be much meat left. Was that even legal? When is waterfowl season anyway? Assuming I could pull that off and it was legal to, what would we make? Do we have jalapeno and cream cheese at camp? I might be able to whip up some poppers. Hmmm, poppers. I'm hungry. I told you, your mind wanders on a sit.

Uncle Manny must have had food on his mind as well. There was no activity at all, so we decided to head back to camp for a cooked lunch rather than eating bars or crackers out of our daypacks.

While eating, we discussed trying a new spot. Maybe the spot closer to camp we saw on the first day? There was this excitement to explore though. Just something in my gut that figured, we are out here, let's see what else there is further down the trail. Uncle Manny was curious as well and we decided that we would go a bit deeper and see what else we could see now that the hunter in the stand that was right off the path would surely be gone.

Rookie lesson number 7: Don't be afraid to change your tactics mid hunt. Go with your gut. It works, you have a successful hunt. If it doesn't you learned something new about your area and maybe your quarry.

After lunch and a quick nap, we walk back out into the woods and we pass the rusty tree stand. We keep walking for another mile or so and we find another clearing. This one was much larger and has a slough to the right, a nice natural choke point, and another slough to the left. As we look down, we can see some fresh deer tracks in the mud and an older panther track. This place looked promising.

We sit near the slough on the right under a small grouping of palm trees and covered by saw palmettos. We start glassing. As we are sitting there for several hours, I whisper to Uncle Manny, "You know what? I would be happy to just see a deer. I don't care if it is a shooter or not, just seeing one would be great." He smiles and nods in agreement.

Last shooting light is upon us and we don't see anything, but we haven't lost faith in the new location. The tracks we saw looked fresh and there was more than one deer crossing that chokepoint. It looked like a very well trafficked game trail. We were cautiously optimistic about the next day.

We only had one more full day to hunt. We had a permit to be out there all week but were only able to get enough days off for a 4-day hunt. However, we would only be able to hunt the morning of the 4th day since we would need to break down camp and head home.

Back at camp we prepare dinner over the fire once again. No matter how close you are to someone, there is something about food and a campfire in the middle of nowhere that gives you a deeper understanding of their personality and character. We share stories and crack jokes before we finally seek shelter from the mosquitos. We get some shut eye for a few hours before its time to hike back out to our new spot.

Chapter 9: Public Land Buck Day 3

We wake up early the next morning with a sense of urgency to get into place in our new spot before daybreak. I notice how easy and natural it feels to quickly fall into the routine of getting up and out on the red headlamp lit walk. The apprehensions I had when I first got out there had eased back into comfortable caution as my familiarity with the landscape and trail grew. This new spot was about

2 and a half miles from camp down the same winding eastward trail.

We get there in about 25 to 30 minutes and the sun still hadn't begun to lighten the sky just yet. We decide to try out the opposite side of the trail from where we had sat the previous day. We find a spot behind a small saw palmetto bush that reached about waist high so we felt once we sat it would break up our silhouette just enough. The chairs we carried out with us this time fit perfectly in between this bush and the tree line at our backs. Uncle Manny sat just behind my left shoulder, enough that I could see his knee out of my peripheral vision if I was looking straight on.

Not long after we get situated, the sky starts to brighten, and the early morning haze begins to clear. Just as the darkness finally fully recedes into a bright and sunny morning, Uncle Manny taps me on the shoulder. I look up, and to our right are two does walking no more than 30 to 40 yards from us. I could feel the light breeze on my face, so I knew they couldn't smell us at all. My phone had been sitting on my lap so I was able to slowly raise it to my chest without breaking my silhouette so I can record them.

The larger of the two does stops and looks directly at us. I can tell that she sees us, but she isn't moving, and neither are we. We are frozen in place.

I am consciously trying to slow my breathing so slow so that even my chest rising wouldn't be as pronounced. This is easier said than done when this is the first deer you have ever seen in the wild. Heck it was the first 4-legged wild animal I had ever seen in the wild period. Sure, I had seen that boar on private land on my first hunt, but this somehow felt purer. I hadn't been guided here. No one told us to look here or sit there. We were in their house and stumbled upon the game trail and strategically sat in this location, and here she was. I am just mouth agape awestruck when she starts to blow and huff at us. My heart races but I don't move. She takes a few steps towards us and stomps on the ground, then blows and huffs again. It was one of the most incredible experiences I had ever had.

She knew something was off about the bush we were sitting in but since we wouldn't move, she didn't bolt. Both does make their way off into the tree line opposite us pausing and looking in our direction every few steps. They slowly make their way off to our left until they finally disappear out of sight around a bend in the tree line.

This right here was worth it. This moment would have been enough for me to come back again. Even if it wasn't a successful hunt, it was a great freaking time. There was no way to describe that feeling. Once they were gone there was a notable sigh from both of us and a whispered chuckle. Uncle Manny then whispered, "There you go, you got to see some deer." I sure had. It almost felt like the edge was off on the trip. I didn't care that it wasn't meat for my freezer, I knew this hunt was a challenging one going in so just seeing deer where they live was enough.

After about an hour of reveling in the morning's experience, it started to get hotter and the sun was beaming down right on top of us. Uncle Manny suggested we back into the tree line and take advantage of some shade. The tree line was pretty thick with brush right where we were sitting, so we decide to walk about 50 yards away from the choke point and around a small bend. We find a hole in the brush that we could walk into and it provided great cover. The canopy of the pine trees above shielded us from the sun and there was a light breeze that made the spot perhaps the best spot we had found this trip. Uncle Manny is now sitting in front of me and off to the left. We get settled in to be here the rest of the day. Being our last day we had decided to not go back to camp for lunch just in case we get lucky.

No more than about 30 to 45 minutes later I am scanning the opposite tree line and notice some movement to my left. As soon as I look in that direction Uncle Manny slowly taps me on the knee. He had picked up on the same movement. A few seconds later a doe and a buck walk right in front of us and stop. There was a slough not more than 30 to 40 yards from us and the buck had stopped to take a sip of water. I slowly grab for my rifle fighting the urge to just snatch it up and shoot. I aim and look for his antlers through my scope. I see two points on either side. It's a forkie! Just as I see that Uncle Manny confirms that it's a shooter and says, "When you are ready, take the shot." He then leans to his left and covers his ears.

I am shooting without a shooting stick or anything to rest my rifle on, but he is close. He is standing broadside so I train my sights on where his lung and heart would be, but His body is obscured by tall sawgrass. I decide to aim for the center of his neck instead. I steady my breathing

Chapter 9: Public Land Buck Day 3

and slowly squeeze the trigger. The roar of the rifle blast is replaced by the splashing of the buck dropping into the slough. The doe runs a few steps and stops to look around. She still had no clue we were there or where the buck was. If we would have had an antlerless deer permit, we would have tagged out that day. It wasn't until we emerged from the tree line that she finally ran off.

The impact of the rifle round had severed its spinal cord and the buck went down instantly. We walked around the area we last saw him and took us a minute to find him in the sawgrass. I was the first to see him and I called over to Uncle Manny, "He is right here!"

Uncle Manny excitedly high steps over to me working his way through the mud and sawgrass. I just stood there staring at my buck. I couldn't believe I had my first deer. It felt surreal. The realization that I had come on my first D.I.Y. public lands hunt and had a deer coming home with me.

Uncle Manny snapped me out of my trance and grabbed hold of one of the buck's antlers and said, "What the hell are you waiting for?" with a huge smirk of pride on his face. He dragged it to a better location to clean it and get it ready for the hike back. I kneel down and just feel his fur and take in the moment. I am grateful for this meat and grateful for the experience. No doubt beginner's luck, but nonetheless, I will take it.

South Florida deer are smaller than the average white tail. From what I understand they are about similar in size as a Coues deer, which are famed for being some of the smallest white-tailed deer. As I am wrapping up the cleaning process Uncle Manny finds a sturdy looking branch on the ground near where we were sitting. It had fallen from a tree but looked sturdy enough to support the deer's weight and was a good length.

Chapter 9: Public Land Buck Day 3

One of the things I had made a point of doing was picking up trash as we walked around. If I am out enjoying the land, I figured the least I could do was help pick up what I find. One of the items I had found was some thin paracord someone had left at the base of one of the pine trees we had sat near. It ended up coming in handy as we tie the deer's legs and head to the long tree branch. As we hoist him up onto our shoulders and feel his weight, Uncle Manny thought it would be a good idea if we left half our gear there so we wouldn't have to haul back so much weight at once. He offered to come back for it while I quartered the deer back at camp.

We then start the 2-and-a-half-mile trek back to camp. We had plenty of daylight, so we had no need to rush getting back. We started strong and took our time, pausing only once initially for a water break. Then my lack of physical fitness started to kick in at the last leg. The normal hike in and out really wasn't too difficult but holding a 120-pound carcass makes every downed branch you walk over more demanding. The inclines and declines in the path feel like more of an obstacle. Your feet get heavier and your hamstrings and thighs sorer with every awkward step you take to maintain balance. We trudge on though. I can finally see the last obstacle before camp. The large pond that blocked the main path. As I think of the small, crowded path we need to navigate to get around it, I decide I need a break before we go through it. Uncle Manny is ready to push through, however. We take a quick minute to drink water and I make a note, I need to get in shape if I want to do a western hunt in the mountains. This is nothing compared to what I imagine it would be like packing out a much larger animal, in much more demanding terrain. Sure, we have mud and muck to deal with, but I can only imagine climbing or descending unsteady terrain with all that extra weight.

We finally make it back to camp and drive the deer on the back of the truck the rest of the way to the warden's hut at the entrance of the unit. There was no one there so we filled out our paperwork to check in the harvest and drop it in the drop box. Uncle Manny drops me back off at our campsite and I get to work while he hikes back down the trail for the rest of our gear.

While quartering it I got a few visits from fellow hunters around camp curious to see who had shot a buck and to give their congratulations. One hunter looked relieved. He had been hunting a 10-point buck he had seen on his trail cams while scouting and was certain I had shot it. One thing I will say, the hunting community in Florida is small, especially in South Florida, but one of the things I love is it is tight knit. You could have never met, but once you each know the other is a hunter, there is something that triggers and pretty much draws you into conversation with one another. I have been in social situations where someone will mention they hunt or were on a hunt and immediately we end up talking to one another for the rest of the event. That is true except on social media. Be careful what you ask on hunting groups, many bozos think its funny to misinform fellow rookie hunters so always take advice with a grain of salt unless you get it from more than one reputable source.

Seeing as we only had the next morning to hunt and would have had to come back and pack up camp anyway, we decided to pack it up that day and head home for some venison steak.

Rookie Lesson number 8: Unlike fish, where the fresher the better tasting, game meat gets better with age. It is edible for sure, but the meat will always be tough right after it is harvested, vs being allowed to age, whether dry aged or wet aged in a vacuum sealed bag.

While the meat was freshly harvested and tough, it was the sweetest tasting steak I had ever had. For the next year I would smile whenever we had a bit of that deer. Every bite was a memory from that hunt. I would share it with close family and friends and prepared it many ways. My family's favorite was braised or a twist on a Cuban recipe for a dish called "Bistec en Casuela" which literally translates to steak in a pot. It is basically venison steaks slowly cooked in a pot with a tomato-based sauce and root vegetables, peppers, and onions. It is served on a bed of jasmine rice. My wife had been apprehensive about eating wild game, but once she had some, it easily became her favorite form of red meat.

Chapter 10: Swamp Ghosts

After having experienced such an incredible hunt in Big Cypress, Uncle Manny and I were excited for a repeat. When the time came for us to put in for our quota permits, we put in for a few new areas, but a repeat of Big Cypress was definitely on our list. After a little over a month, the drawings were announced and as luck would have it, we again drew Big Cypress. While I would have definitely enjoyed exploring new territory in other great management areas or refuges in the state, I was excited to try out our spot

Chapter 10: Swamp Ghosts

for another year and to possibly head in deeper into the unit and further off the beaten path.

Much to the dismay of our wives, we gear up once again. Learning from our mistakes we upgrade our air mattresses to army style cots and we find lighter hunting clothes. We get better camp kitchen gear and plan our meals more carefully. One of the bonuses of having a truck camp is you can stock slightly more perishable foods for dinner and live out of your truck, vs having to hike everything in and live out of your bag. This is especially important as this time we had planned on staying the whole week. We would arrive Saturday and stay through the following Saturday. My ambition was to walk out of there with a buck each.

The day finally arrives. This time Uncle Manny and I agree to meet there. I drive down Saturday, but I have an extra hour and a half to my drive so Uncle Manny gets there early and sets up camp. The closer I get and the more nature and wide-open spaces I see, the more excited I get. The road is now slightly more familiar. I turn down the dirt road that is the last turn until you get into the unit. It's a straight shot for the last 20 or so minutes. As I arrive at the same familiar warden hut and am greeted by the same game warden and 2 other visitors, one checking in, and one who was lost and trying to find a way back to the highway.

Once I have my paperwork all squared away, I call Uncle Manny to get the tent site number and I start down the one lane dirt road. As I am driving, I think to myself, good it looks empty. As much as I like seeing people enjoying public land, I also like having a large portion to myself when hunting. It's a conflicting happiness. I pass the tent site and continue until I reach the end of the dirt road where it turns into the walk-in only path. To my dismay there are trucks parked everywhere. It looked like an off-road meet up. There were a lot of hunters out there. I turn back around and head back to what we would call home for a week.

Chapter 10: Swamp Ghosts

This time our camp was diagonal from the camp we had stayed at the year prior which made us only a few steps further from the entrance to the walk-in only camp. This site was in the shape of a circle with a u attached to the top of it to allow your truck to pull in. It looked like the symbol for the astrological sign Taurus "♉". In the middle of the circle is a group of palm and pine trees with an underbrush of saw palmettos and beauty berries (bush that bears small bright purple berries that are edible, but don't really taste like much of anything. Deer will eat it as a food of last resort).

If you were standing at the top of the u-shaped area and facing the middle of the circle My truck would be to the right, Uncle Manny's would be to the left and a fire pit would be right in front of you. Directly behind Uncle Manny's truck is a large picnic table and behind that towards what would be the left of the circle is our large tent that we would be our bedroom for the week. The tent is a large 8-

person tent in the shape of an igloo. To the left side of the main area of the tent lies my cot, and to the right is Uncle Manny's cot with a camp table in between us that holds our headlamps, sidearms, and bear spray.

Once camp is set up and our food for the evening is sorted we discussed going out and trying to scout, but decided against it since we didn't want to stumble through and bump any deer away from any of the hunters that are already out there during last shooting light. We wrap a few steaks and chopped potatoes in aluminum foil and throw it onto a metal grate just above the firepit. After dinner we head into the tent just as the night starts to take over and get some shut eye before a very early morning.

***

While we were sleeping a cold front had started to roll through and the temperatures dropped to 54

Chapter 10: Swamp Ghosts

degrees. Now I realize to most folks up north that is beautiful weather, but to a south Florida grown boy like myself, that was teeth chattering cold and I was not prepared. The year prior had been abnormally hot and humid, and even the week prior to this hunt we had seen temps in the mid to upper 80s.

I layer up the best I can with the thin cotton shirts I had brought expecting hot weather and we hit the trail. As we approach the trail head there were two trucks already parked with their owners already in the woods. This was approximately 5AM. I feel a little pang of disappointment that we won't be the only ones out there. The trail head looked a little different. There was no rusted locked gate blocking vehicles anymore despite there still being a sign indicating this was still a walk-in only trail. The pond was still there and the side trail we used to go around it was a little more overgrown but still there as well. The path is familiar which gives me a level of comfort and confidence I didn't have the last time I was here. I could tell there was something different in the landscape even in this darkness, but despite that my feet still knew where they were headed.

We were going to bypass the rusty tree stand this time and start where our last trip ended. We were going to that large open area with the natural chokepoint. We walk the 2 miles or so in mostly silence just taking it all in. As we approach our spot, the edges of the sky just behind the tops of the trees is starting to turn from black to a blueish grey as the sun is starting to rise and pierce the darkness.

The night starts to fade into day, and I can see that there was some sort of fire in the area. The canopy that was once there from the pine trees is gone and the underbrush is much thicker. The saw palmettos have grown bigger and more intertwined and bushier with the added sunlight. We head over to roughly the same area we saw the buck last time and settle in. The day was cold and grey and eerily

Chapter 10: Swamp Ghosts

quiet. At about mid-morning I hear some rustling behind my right shoulder near the trail we had veered from. I slowly turn hoping to see deer, but unfortunately, what I see is a group of 3 hunters potentially trying out a new spot further up the trail.

The morning haze never really cleared up and it remained a steel grey the rest of the day. It warmed up a few degrees before the breeze kicked in again in the afternoon urging the temperature to drop yet again. We had stayed out in our spot all day with no activity other than the birds flying overhead. Some interesting ones like blue herons and kingfishers, and some more common like crows and boat tailed grackles. There are obvious signs of deer passing through. There are deep tracks in the soft mud around us and clear trails made from constant use in the sawgrass. The rest of the day is quiet except for a few far-off rifle shots that remind us that there are still a good number of hunters in the area. Sunset finally rolls around quietly so we decide to head back to camp.

Once we arrive, I begin preparing one of my favorite camp meals. Garbanzo Frito, or Fried Chickpeas. It is Spanish sausage, bacon, onions, and chickpeas fried together in a cast iron skillet over my propane gas burner. If you don't have the luxury of a truck camp, this is still a good recipe minus the bacon as all of the ingredients keep very well without needing to be refrigerated. Even the Spanish sausage is cured and in a vacuum sealed package so it will keep for a while as long as the temps aren't too hot. In a pinch you could substitute the bacon with beef jerky, but I would use one with a smokey or neutral flavor, stay away from stronger flavors like teriyaki.

Over dinner we take a look at a satellite image of our spot and see some other areas that look like they may have some potential. We decide we would try setting up the next morning across the clearing and slough about 200 yards from where we sat that day. We also mark a waypoint about 300 yards to the north which has a view with a whole other clearing and slough that isn't visible from our spot.

***

We wake up the next morning after a long night shivering through the cold. I make a mental note to buy some cold weather camping gear for the future.

Rookie lesson number 9: *Make sure to check the weather before you head out hunting. I know, seems like a no brainer, but it is easy to get caught up in what you imagine for the trip and forget to check what it actually will be like.*

We hit the now familiar trail again and set up where we had discussed the night before. On the way in this time, we notice there were no trucks and no sign of other hunters. For now, at least, it looks like we have the walk-in area to ourselves. The view from our new set up looks very different. We have a much wider view of the clearing we were hunting. We can see over 700 yards straight ahead of us, and that distance quickly tapers off as you follow the tree line to either side. It is as if we are sitting on the point of a triangle. The trees and brush outline the rest of the triangle with 2 large sloughs making up the middle. The sides of the triangle are slightly bowed, and the bottom of the triangle has a gap that leads into another clearing. That gap however is obscured by tall grass and brush. To our back right is an open area that forms a semicircle until it reaches another natural chokepoint which opens into another clearing and a smaller slough.

There are plenty of clearly visible game trails in the area. The sawgrass is so long you would think it would conceal the trails, but they seem to be so highly travelled that the grass actually does the opposite and accentuates the game trails so that they are clearly visible and look like tire tracks on a highway.

Chapter 10: Swamp Ghosts

The breeze today is much lighter. So light, that at times it can be quite difficult to tell if the wind is in our favor or not. Uncle Manny pulls a thread off his shemagh and ties it to a tree branch. It is so light that it immediately dances in the direction the wind is pushing it. We were good, the wind is carrying our scent straight back behind us where the brush is so thick it would be difficult to see any deer in that direction anyway, much less get a good shot.

Rookie lesson number 10: Wind is one of the most important factors to keep in mind and one of the easiest for a new hunter to forget. It can easily change over time and do so subtly. Even a light breeze can carry your scent to a deer that will avoid you without you ever having heard or seen them. You keep wind in mind, it can be your biggest asset when hunting, forget about it and it can turn into your biggest obstacle.

The day is as quiet, yet much more beautiful, than the previous day. The front had passed and taken all those grey clouds with it. The sky was an incredible deep blue and the grasses and bushes around us were all shades of greens and yellows. The cool air was a welcome change to the mosquito ridden humidity from the first time we hunted the area.

The day goes on quietly without any deer, but also, no people. About midday we decide to take a slow walk further up the path to scout out if there are any other good areas even though we still feel pretty good about this spot.

We make our way back to the trail and take a left to head east, away from camp. As soon as we do, the trail quickly narrows and turns into more of a narrow footpath. The signs of the brush fire in the area are even more apparent as the path is obscured by downed blackened trees and long black charcoal logs that were once pine trees standing amidst what is now the bright new green growth. I can't believe how much a landscape can

Chapter 10: Swamp Ghosts

change in just a year. Not just how much it can change, but how quickly nature can regain its foothold and breathe new life.

We try to walk quietly but the path is covered in burnt twigs and branches that snap as we walk, or with thick mud that makes it difficult for you to quietly keep your balance and tries to suck off your boots with every step. As we turn one corner, we bump a turkey which jets across the path in front of us and ducks into the bushes on the opposite side of the narrow trail.

We finally emerge into a new clearing that is much smaller than where we had been before. It is surrounded by large cypress trees many of which had ankle deep water around their base. It is an interesting area but there are much less signs of deer here. We could have kept passed the cypress to see more but we notice that the clearing opens up to the right of the trail. We decide to follow the tree line to see where it leads. After just a few steps the clearing opens up again and we are now standing at the northernmost end of a large circular clearing that has a diameter of about 300 yards. What was most interesting though was that there were bedding areas and as many, if not more, game trails than where we were sitting earlier that morning. We still feel pretty good about our spot, so we decide to give it one more day there before we try this new spot.

We head back to the tip of the triangle we were sitting at in the morning and spend the rest of the afternoon enjoying the view and waiting for deer that never show. The deer sign are many though so we aren't ready to give up just yet. At camp we decide to give it one more day before changing our strategy.

***

The next morning seems even quieter still than the day before. The weather is still crisp and cool,

Chapter 10: Swamp Ghosts

and the trailhead is once again empty, much to our delight. We head down the familiar trail yet again. We set up at the tip of the triangle again. This time though, just before the sun fully takes over the morning and the early haze lifts, I hear sloshing around in the slough. Just a few seconds pass and a young spike buck emerges from the sawgrass 100 yards from us. I tap Uncle Manny on the shoulder and quietly point in the buck's direction. He looks at him through his scope and confirms it is a spike and not a legal buck.

As the buck starts walking toward the tree line opposite of us, 2 more bucks emerge. I start to feel that familiar feeling. My heart starts to speed up and internally the buck fever starts to take hold while I consciously make an effort to control its impacts externally. Uncle Manny and I both look through our scopes as both bucks have antlers that look long enough to be legal. As we look through the scope however, both seem to only have a single point. Astonishing given that one's antlers was at least a foot long.

Rookie lesson number 11: Many states and properties have rules on antler size for what is a legal to take buck or not. It is hard to tell from a distance and through a scope what the length of an antler is. So, to help, it is good to keep in mind that the measurement from a deer's eye to the tip of their nose is on average 7 to 8 inches. The measurement from the tip of one ear to the opposite ear is generally 13 to 15 inches. So, when gauging the size of the antler, it is good to use those two measurements as a reference.

Sure enough though, we could only spot the single point at the top of the antler and no other visible points. We just keep watching the deer until suddenly and just as quickly as they had shown up, they had slid into the saw palmetto brush on the opposite tree line and disappeared. It was quick and quiet, so much so that you almost doubt having seen it.

The rest of the day was the same as the last two. We decide to split up to cover more ground and have a better chance at taking home meat for our freezers. The next few days were filled with similar experiences. Quick glimpses of both doe and bucks that were not legal to harvest. They would appear and disappear just as suddenly each time.

Then, as soon as Friday came around more trucks appeared, more hunters were in the area, and the deer were just gone. This year the deer were ghosts only granting us brief glimpses and interactions. Enough to tease your excitement and keep you hoping. Then just like that, it was as if they were never there.

Rookie lesson number 12: *Don't underestimate the impact of too many hunters afield. Weekends of course will always be the* *busiest days on any given piece of public land. If possible, try hunting during the middle of the week. You will have a much higher chance at finding your quarry than on the weekend. Now as I say that, if all you have is the weekend, by all means head out! Don't let the number of hunters out there scare you away either. It is possible that a hunter can bump a deer over to you accidentally, or you just happen to be at the right place at the right time.*

We headed home on Saturday afternoon empty handed. Even so it was an incredible experience. I still treasured those brief glimpses and being out in the woods disconnected and sharing that time with one of my closest buddies. There was no meat for our freezer, but we also left with no regrets and came home with an awesome experience.

Chapter 11: Passing the Torch

As I had been growing more and more enamored with the outdoors and gaining experience hunting, my brother in law, Pedro, was growing more and more curious. Pedro is tall, about 6'1" or 6'2" and is lean with thick black curly hair which he keeps cut short and clean cut, the opposite of the goatee he has been growing ever since he left the Army. It was getting quite long and scraggly. He was serving overseas in Germany while I was learning the ropes and I would recount the experiences to him on our calls or over WhatsApp messages. He would get excited for me and ask all kinds of questions like what did it feel like, and how did I like the taste of wild game, and how would he be able to hunt when he got home? The curiosity in him only grew when he was stationed in Georgia for the last leg of his enlistment. It was funny hearing him excitedly ask me question after question and I could imagine him picturing himself on a hunt as I answered. It reminded me of how I felt when I asked the same questions of Uncle Manny and Leon before my first hunt.

Once he got his final papers he came home to concentrate on school for a while. On one occasion he had asked if I had any wild game left from one of my previous hunts, as a matter of fact I did! I was on my last few cuts of meat. I told him I would make him something so he could try it and see if he liked it. I reached into my freezer and pulled out a blade roast I had been saving. I decided I was going to prepare it one of my favorite ways of preparing wild game. I season the roast with a dry rub I had put

Chapter 11: Passing the Torch

together with some spices from my cabinet and some herbs from my garden. I then sear it on all sides in a Dutch oven over some peanut oil. Once seared, I remove the roast and toss in onions, peppers, and garlic along with some Worcestershire sauce to help deglaze the bottom of the pot and help give an added flavor to the now caramelizing peppers and onions. Once the peppers gain a glazed appearance, I put the roast back in the pot and add some root vegetables (potatoes and carrots in this case but also goes well with turnips). I then fill the pot with broth or water until it covers half to three quarters of the roast. I then cover it and throw it in the oven at 275 to 300 degrees. After a few hours, depending on the size of the roast, the meat is fall off the bone tender. I served it to him over a bed of jasmine rice.

The minute I had pulled the roast out of the oven, he was perched on my shoulder. He said the smell had been driving him nuts for hours. My wife serves the family and we sit at the table to eat. As soon as the first forkful hits his taste buds, he looks at me and says, "Bert! When are you taking me hunting?"

We talked about figuring out when and where to go hunt when the season rolled around. I told him how to get his hunter safety card and how to apply for his license, when one of his buddies from his last post called him up. His family had purchased a small ranch in central Texas, and he wanted to invite us to go on a hunt. We could hunt hogs with no problem, and his dad would allow one of us to hunt a doe. Pedro was ecstatic and even though it was last minute it was too big of an opportunity to say no. The date was going to be a little hectic to swing because a hunt I did have planned would start the following weekend and I couldn't take too many days off work, nor could Pedro miss any school. That meant we would leave Thursday evening after work and come back Monday.

Being last minute we decided to drive the whole way as airline tickets were just too pricey. Also, I

Chapter 11: Passing the Torch

had never had to travel with rifles and, if we were successful, raw meat. We decided the logistics were too complicated to figure out with such a small notice, so the decision came down to his truck or mine.

It would be an 18-hour drive to Dallas to link up with his buddy John. We would then load our gear into his Chevy, and he would drive us the final 5 hours to his family ranch.

Pedro got to my house at about 8PM. He was already wired and hopped up on an energy drink he chugged down on the way over. We hastily loaded up the rifles and gear into the back of his truck and said our goodbyes to my wife and kids. He had first shift so after catching up a bit I grabbed some shut eye while he drove. We would alternate the whole drive up and back, with Pedro taking the lion's share of the driving. He is the son of a trucker and can zone out on long drives as if it were an inherited trait.

The drive there felt shorter than we thought it would be. As we were entering Texas, we happened to have passed by several large 18 wheelers transporting caged chickens. They were full grown and being the proud owner of backyard chickens myself, I recognized them as Cornish cross chickens. This breed of chicken is technically man made. They have been bred for rapid growth. They will reach market weight of 4 to 6 lbs by the time they are only 8 weeks old. To put this into perspective, the average hen will start laying eggs at 6 months old. These chickens will continue to put on weight until their legs can no longer support them and they will often begin to die. They are referred to as meat birds. I can't speak intellectually on the practices of the poultry industry but as we drove passed these trucks I couldn't help but think, I will take a buck or a boar that lived their life in the woods over one of those chickens any day. Unfortunately, I am not lucky enough to have had a

Chapter 11: Passing the Torch

bountiful year to live off solely wild game, but if I could, I would in a heartbeat.

We finally made it to Dallas by early Friday afternoon. John greeted us in the driveway and though I had spoken to him a few times, I had never met him in person. John was a lean guy about average height, but his most distinguishing feature was a long Viking beard he had grown since leaving the Army. These guys take their DD-214 facial hair seriously. John is just an all-around good guy. I mean he wouldn't think twice about giving a friend the shirt off his back.

He had his SUV open and was already organizing his bags and getting some space open for ours. We load up the coolers and bags first and then the rifles on top. Within minutes we were on the road. The drive again felt shorter than it actually was. It was filled with conversation and quite a few jokes.

By the time we arrived at the ranch it was dark out. The road leading to the ranch was a long and winding dirt road with ranchland on either side interrupted by large bushes and trees every few feet. As we approached, we could see deer after deer running alongside us for a few steps before veering off into the darkness again. We must have seen at least 7 or 8 deer on the way in. at least 2 of them had 6 to 8-point racks on their head. I couldn't believe my eyes.

We pull up to the driveway of the main house on the ranch where Mr. Buron, John's dad, was waiting for us. He was approximately the same height as John and had salt and pepper hair and a light grey beard that was trimmed and neat.

Mr. Buron had bought this ranch as a family getaway in the country. He practices quality deer management on the property and is very detailed and meticulous in how the ranch was maintained. He is a great steward of his land and maintains a

Chapter 11: Passing the Torch

record of the wildlife that calls his property home. This record is turned in to the Texas Parks and Wildlife Department which helps them with research, quality habitat management, and tracking. Basically, I kind of want to grow up to be like Mr. Buron.

He sets us up in two guest bedrooms and told us where we would be hunting the next morning. Mr. Buron had told John about what looked to be a 10-point buck he had captured on the trail cams. John had also seen a buck that interested him that we had called the claw. It was tough to tell how many points he had but there was an interesting formation on one side in which two points grew in the shape of a lobster claw. We would be able to hunt all day Saturday and Sunday and then head back to Dallas on Monday to pick up Pedro's truck and then it was straight back to Loxahatchee for me and Miami for Pedro.

Since it would be Pedro's first hunt, I told him the doe would be for him and I would only take a hog if he had already been successful. This hunt was for Pedro, not for me. We couldn't hunt doe during the morning hunt because we had gotten there so late, we hadn't picked up a permit yet. Hog, on the other hand, needs no permit on private property.

We wake up at about 5AM the next morning. It is forecast to be in the 40s in the morning but jumps right back up to the low 70s in the afternoon. Both Pedro and I are not used to the weather, so we layer up pretty good, grab a hot cup of coffee and are ready to go. Mr. Buron drives us out to the stand in a UTV he had parked out front. It is a gas UTV and all I could think of was, aren't we going to bump all the deer? As we drove, I can see deer running off into the darkness avoiding the UTV much like they were avoiding the truck the night before as we were driving in. I just couldn't believe how many deer there were in the area. This was not a high fence ranch, the fences that marked the

Chapter 11: Passing the Torch

property line were only about 4 feet tall. Deer can easily clear it and cross in and out of the property into neighboring properties.

We stop about 40 yards from the blind we would be hunting from and walk the rest of the way to it. The floor sits about 6 feet off the ground and fits two people comfortably. Pedro and I climb in and get situated. The main house is several hundred yards to our right and directly in front of us is a feeder at about 100 yards. We had about 120 degrees of safe shooting area. Behind us was a creek that we could hear water sloshing and running through. While we knew all of that was around us, we couldn't yet see the feeder because it was still about 45 minutes before sunrise.

After about 20 minutes, the sky begins to lighten. The darkness begins giving way to a purplish hue that slowly blends into a reddish orange on the horizon. As the sky begins to slowly brighten, we start hearing movement before we see it. Then out of a bush to our right steps out a gorgeous 8-point buck. He is incredible. It is the biggest deer I had ever seen. He just casually strolls on in front of us at no more than 40 yards. Just strutting as if in a fashion show. He walks over to a low hanging branch that is hanging from a tree diagonally from us. He proceeds to urinate and scratch at the ground marking a scrape and then angrily rubs his antlers on the low hanging branch before just as casually as he came into view, he walks off.

Pedro and I let go of a sigh as he left as if we had been holding our breath the whole time. He excitedly whispers to me, "Did you fucking just see that!"

"I sure did. That was incredible" I whispered back.

I had snapped a few pictures of the buck. I really was wishing we could hunt a buck after seeing that. The rest of the morning was filled with numerous

Chapter 11: Passing the Torch

does and at least 2 other bucks. Not as big bodied and impressive, but with beautiful antlers just the same. One of them had walked to within 5 yards of the blind. It was an unreal experience seeing so many deer just nonchalantly carry on.

In his own blind at the top of a large hill on the property sat John. He had a quiet morning and hadn't seen any deer until just as morning finally broke and the sun was shining, the claw had walked right out in front of him. The only problem? He had 8, maybe 9 points if you counted a smaller one on the right antler. Mr. Buron had told him he wanted him to get the 10-pointer. So, while he had the claw in his scope, he didn't pull the trigger. He debated and argued with himself for what he said felt like an eternity until he finally let him pass.

By midday the activity had all but ceased. John walked up just as Pedro and I were climbing out of the blind. We shared our experiences and he proceeded to take us on a tour of the property. We went down into a ditch that led us to the creek which is right up near the edge of their property. There were plenty of tracks in the soft mud on the banks of the creek. It was clear that this was a common watering hole. We walked the bank for a bit before climbing back up onto the area we had been hunting in the morning.

Behind the feeder is what looks like an old dried up creek bed and then there is a clearing that leads up to the huge hill where John had been hunting from in the morning. We hopped on a UTV John had rode over to us in and we picked up Mr. Buron and some 40-pound bags of corn so we could help him refill feeders. The property is quite large, but I think my favorite area was at the top of the hill. It overlooked most of the surrounding area which gave it incredible views of neighboring ranches and hunting properties. Another place that came close was a small area tucked away at the far end of their property that was filled with acorn trees. The trees formed a kind of canopy and there was a carpet of

Chapter 11: Passing the Torch

dried leaves and acorns strewn about that left the ground with all shades of reds, oranges, and browns.

After refilling all the feeders and touring the property, John and Mr. Buron take us into town to get that permit and non-resident hunting license for Pedro. Also, the town had a barbecue place that John had been talking up for the few weeks before we got there. Let me say, the barbecue did not disappoint. It was one of the best briskets I had ever had. It had just the right amount of smokiness, tenderness, and juiciness. We recount our morning to Mr. Buron and John tells him about his interaction with the claw. He tells John "You should have shot him!"

John laughs and tells him "I thought you wanted me to get the 10-pointer."

"I do, but that's a good one too." He replied.

"Dammit, I knew I should have taken the shot!" John replied instantly regretting his decision that morning. Pedro and I comment that he should see him again, he is obviously in the area and likes that feeder as evidenced by the game cameras. Mr. Buron graciously treats us to lunch and we head back to the ranch so that we can be in the blind and settled way before sunset.

As soon as the sky starts to slightly dim, the activity starts to pick up again around the blind. We see a grey fox doing a little hunting of his own. He was hot on the trail of something as he trotted past at about 15 yards. To our right we can see 3 does feeding in a field at about 50 to 70 yards. We don't target any of these because we wanted to make sure didn't get a doe that was partnered with other does or potentially fawns. Given that this was not a place we would be suffering to find deer, we would wait for the right one. Again, we see a few bucks that stroll through. Then, right at sunset, we get our eyes on a lone doe by the feeder. She wasn't the

Chapter 11: Passing the Torch

biggest we had seen, but she was alone, which was the main thing we were looking out for. We wanted to respect all the hard work Mr. Buron had put in to managing this herd.

As I spot her, I whisper to Pedro, "There she is."

"You sure? That's a good one?" he nervously replied, not believing he was moments away from his first successful harvest.

"Yup, she is alone. Doesn't look too big, but the first one I see that's alone so far. Is she good enough for you?"

A simple but excited "Yes!" was his reply.

"Ok remember we are aiming just behind her shoulder. She is broad side so that should put it right in the area of her lungs and heart. Shoot whenever you are ready."

Pedro takes a deep breath and looks for her in his scope. I can hear him try and steady his breathing. I can see him slowly start to squeeze the trigger until BANG, the rifle barks and the doe jumps what looks like 10 feet in the air and disappears behind a bush.

Simultaneously he whispers "Shit! I missed" and I whisper, "Perfect shot!"

"Nah man I missed her; I know I did." The color leaves his face and you can see the disappointment wash over him.

"I don't think so, it looked like perfect placement to me dude. Let's give her a minute before we go check just in case."

Rookie lesson number 13: Thankfully this one I learned early on and never had to learn the hard way. Not all shots are clean. No matter how much you practice, no matter how conservative you are

Chapter 11: Passing the Torch

about the shots you take, there may come a time that you don't have the best placement. This can mean a lost animal, or can mean mortally wounding one, but may take them some time to pass. It is not ideal, and not desirable in any way, but it happens. Never rush out to the animal, especially if it is a buck. An injured animal is scared and may instinctively attack. If you can put the animal out of its misery, then by all means, do it, but always keep your safety in mind. Also, if possible, always approach from behind the animal, not from in front.

After a few minutes, we climb out of the blind. We slowly walk in the direction of the bush we had last seen the doe. I am a few steps ahead of Pedro, so I was the first to see the soft tan and white belly of the doe laying on the ground.

"There she is!"

"No man, stop playing around." Pedro replied, but with every step we took closer the more his face changed and curled into a smile. By the time we reached the doe, he was beaming, and the smile was from ear to ear. He kneeled and slowly pet her fur. I let him take it all in for a few minutes before we carried her to a UTV and drove her back to the main house where there was a cleaning station. I walked Pedro through the cleaning process, and he got his deer quartered and iced. The whole experience was incredible for me as well. It felt as though I were reliving my first hunt in a third person view. Seeing the doubt of the shot placement, the fear of letting the animal suffer, and then the excitement of knowing that the shot placement was perfect and that you have a cooler full of meat. It is indescribable.

John unfortunately did not get another chance at the claw or the 10-pointer that was on the game cam pictures. It wasn't until a month later that John had sealed the deal and finally came across the claw again. He sent us a picture and that was it. No comment or witty caption as the picture spoke for

Chapter 11: Passing the Torch

itself. He had sealed the deal. Then the replies from me and Pedro were instantaneous and filled with genuine excitement and happiness for him.

I never did get my hands on a Texas hog that trip. That didn't matter though. Pedro got his deer and we had an incredible time with John and his dad. It's a trip I won't ever forget, and I know Pedro will never forget.

AFTERWARD

t's no small thing to take a life, any life. I could give all the textbook answers about conservation but that wouldn't be effective in explaining hunting to new or non-hunters. If you are a meat eater, especially if you are a foodie that enjoys preparing your own food and enjoying gourmet meals, there is no closer relationship you can have with what you eat than by hunting your own meat. When you bite into wild game you taste more than the food. You savor and revel in the experiences and hard work that went into obtaining that meal. You taste the rollercoaster ride of missed shot opportunities, good and bad decisions, and

AFTERWARD

finally, despite all of that, a successful hunt. It gives you a whole new perspective on where your food comes from. The animals I hunt are incredibly beautiful and majestic. They also provide my family with meat. In that lies this gruesome yet beautiful circle of life that is inescapable.

I realize hunting is not for everyone, but if you eat meat today, I encourage you to give it a try. There is a purity in the experience that I can't quite put into words. It's easy to go to the grocery store and pick up that neatly plastic wrapped package with clean cuts of protein, and never give a thought to how that meat got there. It is easy to not think of the animal that gave its life after living on a farm or ranch for your next meal. The level of appreciation and gratitude for my food has grown 10-fold because of hunting. I hope this book has answered questions you may have had or inspired you to take the leap and get your hunting license this year. Good luck and I hope to see you on the trail.

Author's Notes

My knowledge and understanding of wildlife mentioned in this book comes from information put out by the Florida Fish and Wildlife Commission, National Wildlife Federation, Encyclopedia Britannica, livescience.com, and the U.S. Fish and Wildlife Service.

My knowledge and understanding of hunting tips and lessons have come from personal experience, advice from my mentor, the Meat Eater TV show as well as articles and podcasts from themeateater.com. Other sources of information that have impacted my knowledge have been Field & Stream magazine, and the wired to hunt blog.

Books that have inspired me to get out and enjoy the outdoors and have also shaped my knowledge and understanding have been *Meat Eater Adventures from the Life of an American Hunter* by Steven Rinella, *The River of Doubt* By Candice Millard, *The Oregon Trail* by Francis Parkman Jr., *American Buffalo In Search of a Lost Icon* By Steven Rinella, and *That Wild Country* by Mark Kenyon.

www.ingramcontent.com/pod-product-compliance
Lightning Source LLC
Chambersburg PA
CBHW032112280326
41933CB00009B/802